Whispers Beneath the Orange Grove

Yaffa

Copyright © Yaffa AS
Published in 2024 by Meraj Publishing
Illustrations copyright © 2024

All rights reserved.
This is a work of creative nonfiction and memoir. It reflects the author's present recollections of experiences over time. Some names and characteristics have been changed, some events have been compressed, and some dialogue has been recreated.

No part of this book or associated artwork may be reproduced or used in any manner without written permission of the publisher or author, except as permitted by copyright law. For more information, address: **info@merajpublishing.com**

ISBN: 979-8-9894734-5-8
First paperback edition October 2024
Book cover by Yaffa AS
Line Edited by Mays Salamah
Formatting by Andrea Ramos Campos

merajpublishing.com

To the people whose lives require trigger warnings.
May we be the trigger for the revolution.

Previous publications by Yaffa:

Blood Orange

Inara: Light to Utopia

Desecrated Poppies

There is No Good Settler Colony..................5
Collectivism............................. 15
Community Care as Practice...............29
On Strategy............................ 59
When They Come for Us......................79
We Move Underground............................93
Letting Go............................... 107
Yearning for Utopia............................. 117
Acknowledgements............................137

There is No Good Settler Colony

There is No Good Settler Colony

Being in israel, like being in the united states, like being in canada, like being in northern Ireland is being in an alternate reality, where oppression is celebrated and the most basic of ethics are invisible. Almost everything is invisible, unless you look a certain way and you act a certain way and you feel a certain way and then you are introduced into the miasma of violence that exists at every turn.

As a Palestinian in israel, easily racialized as such, israelis have taken every opportunity to say the following words as if it is part of their constitution—it is:

"I hope every woman and child is killed in Gaza and Lebanon and we make them us."

There is no mention of Hamas or men, just the total annihilation of the future. Almost word for word in taxis, at the beach, coffee shops, borders, and train stations these are uttered, recognizing that as a Palestinian, there is nothing I can do about it. Even just sharing it publicly can result in indefinite administrative detention where I will be tortured, raped, starved, and potentially killed. This is the fear and reality that every Palestinian in Palestine experiences daily.

It might seem as if the other settler colonies listed above are havens in comparison. However, I have spent half my life in various states in what's knows as the united states where I am told my people deserve genocide. I heard the same in canada. The british of northern Ireland told me that my people deserve to die because the Irish liked us and I needed to be erased through conversion therapy for being "God's mistake." canada told me that to be a refugee I had to say that I support israel, even as a child.

There is no good settler colony. There can never be when they are built on so much death that we will never know exact numbers killed, built on sexual violence that has left no one untouched, built from pillaging land and driving us into climate catastrophe.

There is no good settler colony.

On this one year anniversary of October 7th, I am back in Turtle Island after having been home for the very first time—something I did not expect to happen until a liberated Falasteen welcomes me home. Instead, I navigated borders built to keep my family out for over 76 years. And due to the supplier of all the funds for my people's genocide, I walked in, the first from my immediate family in over 60 years—as the rest of the family who stayed are killed in every war and genocide.

I am emptying my apartment on Ohlone land, sending prayers and gratitude to the ancestors and caretakers of this land as I prepare to leave. I prepare to leave to the closest I can get to my ancestral land, to caretake for land that would otherwise be developed by capitalist vultures who do not care for the land or any of us who reside on it. I am grateful for the years I was forced to live on this land, not due to any loyalty or gratitude to the settler colony cannibalizing it, but due to the relationships I have built with the land, and with Trans, Black, and Indigenous caretakers of the land. I am grateful and I will continue fighting until Turtle Island and everywhere else I have been to and lived in are free.

I can not in good conscience talk about the realities of Gaza without acknowledging the realities of settler colonialism everywhere. There is no independent settler colony, they rise and die interlinked.

There is no good settler colony.

Settler colonies can not exist without the support of other settler colonies as well as colonial entities and their settlers. Ultimately, it is settlers that keep the systems running, whether intentionally or unintentionally.

Sitting in Haifa, watching settlers walk by, I feel no different than sitting in oakland and watching white people walk by. Until we acknowledge the realities of settler hood within settler colonies we can not free ourselves and our people.

We also can not pretend as if our experiences of genocide make us incapable of uplifting systems of oppression and becoming settlers ourselves, harming other Indigenous communities. Without that acknowledgement, we are trying to dismantle a settler colony by strengthening another, ultimately keeping the status quo. We must acknowledge settler hood and the realities of experiences beyond single identities.

In the last year, I have have seen anti-Blackness, anti-Transness, anti-Muslim, anti-Disability hatred weaponized in all directions, within and outside the Pro-Palestine movement. The reality is that there are Palestinians who are pro-genocide, there are Black people who are pro-genocide, there are Trans people who are pro-genocide. There are Palestinians who are anti-Black (including anti-Black Palestinians and Black Palestinians being anti-Black). There are Black people who are anti-Palestinian (anti-Muslim and xenophobic). There are Trans people who are anti-everyone.

The list goes on and on. Pretending otherwise is to pretend as if we are not impacted by systems of oppression, as if we are not punished when we stand for justice and rewarded when we carry the master's tools.

One year into this genocide, I can focus on the hundreds of thousands of Palestinians from Gaza who have been killed, the over ten thousand political prisoners, the thousands killed in what's known as the West Bank. I can focus on Lebanon and Iran. But none of it matters if we don't acknowledge the realities of what and who invades our movements like termites, forcing us to rebuild again and again. We are back to rebuilding.

Every Muslim who was in the united states during and post-9/11 knows every single one of our spaces have been infiltrated by the FBI, whether it's a mosque, a support group, Islamic school, non-profit, or even a kindergarten. We also know that FBI infiltration (cointelpro) did not start with 9/11 and it never ended with Muslims. Every one of our movements is infiltrated, especially the spaces that threaten the empire most, such as transformative and restorative justice spaces.

This infiltration pairs well with community members who are conditioned to systems of oppression our entire lives. That conditioning requires intentional unlearning and deconditioning to move past.

Liberation is not systems of oppression ceding to exist, liberation is recognizing the power that systems of oppression have been telling us we do not have. Systems of oppression can punish us in every way but they are terrified of our power. The most marginalized of the most marginalized are the people who know this best. When you're so far in the margins of marginalization that assimilation is not possible at all, you are forced to come to terms with this reality.

Recognizing that we are powerful is critical and is one of the most threatening things to empire. If we already recognized this then the revolution would already be here.

Here is the reality, Kamala will not get into office without the most marginalized of the most marginalized. A free Falasteen will not happen without the most marginalized at the forefront. This cycle will not end. Not addressing anti-Blackness is empowering zionism. Not addressing Trans hate is empowering zionism. Not addressing white supremacy is empowering zionism. Not addressing settler hood is empowering zionism. We must stop empowering zionism and instead need to empower Black, Palestinian, Disabled, Indigenous, Trans, and other marginalized communities. I do not say individuals anymore, for this is about community. Supporting individuals is tokenization at best.

I was asked at a recent event how we ensure that there is no vacuum when Falasteen is free. My answer is always by centering, investing, and empowering the most marginalized of the most marginalized. However, if we are not careful the most marginalized are the first to burn out and die (or be killed), the first to disappear, and when the revolution is over, there are only people who look and feel a lot like our oppressors, continuing cycles of oppression.

There will never be a good settler colony, even if the people running it believe they are good.

Ultimately, there are no good settlers within settler colonies. Settlers on stolen land trying to save Indigenous people on another land—who don't recognize and acknowledge their settler hood and the role they play in the demise of Indigenous sovereignty—will never be the answer. They will never be the most marginalized of the most marginalized.

May the world envisioned by the most marginalized of the most marginalized usher in an age of liberation and Indigenous sovereignty.

Collectivism

Collectivism

I was recently reminded of Alma, the Palestinian twelve-year-old in Gaza buried under rubble who begged paramedics to help her family unless they needed her to help them. It reminded me of being 6, praying during Taraweeh and a person telling me I prayed so well and they would buy me candy. This sounds like the beginning of a horror movie, but instead I was the one following this person around for days until they went next door and finally bought me candy. I saw him once, 6 years later and I refused to acknowledge that I remembered him, because I felt I had been too demanding even though he was the one who promised the candy. When I got into the car I handed the candy to my sisters, making sure all four got some, because what I didn't know how to name back then is that they would not have known to share it, but I did. In fact, I was the last to eat from the candy.

I could blame my mom's anxiety for this on one hand. Her terror every time one of the sisters was out of sight for a moment. On the other hand, I think I've always been here for collectivism.

At 22 months old, I remember crying knowing my grandmother was dying in the room behind me. My uncle threatened me into silence and I immediately allowed myself to disassociate. I didn't disassociate for self-preservation, I disassociated because I knew I was disrupting a beautiful event that I did not fully understand yet.

Several months later, as we were doing my younger sister's first medical check up at a clinic, I saw a door wide open. I left, heading for Saudi Arabia. I never understood why. At such a young age why did I have such a deep impulse to escape? Writing this essay, I am realizing it was to not be a burden. I ran away dozens—if not hundreds of times over the years after that.

I wasn't expecting to move the conversation towards burdens and collectivism. I did feel like a burden and thus valued everyone around me more. Their wellness was more important than mine. I even left home to "save their lives" according to my psychosis when I was 17.

In a way, my sense of self was built as an extension of community and there was never a day where I was an individual.

A few months ago, Mama had mentioned to me that I have always done things for everyone else. She didn't just mean taking care of others; she had finally witnessed that every aspect of my life was in one way or another for others. I do not do things I do not want to do, but when things happen, where and how I take action is always strategic and is about community building.

As I write this, I am in a coffee shop in Oslo. The area I am in is more white than what I have become familiar with in Gronland, home to the Global Majority community that invited me here. My eye makeup game here is on fire, and I am wearing a "queers for a free Palestine" shirt made by the fabulous team behind New Orleans Freedom Forum (thank you Thafer).

I am the only one wearing gorgeous makeup, earrings—overall fabulousness. I am also the only person (legitimately) who wears masks indoors. From the thousands I have seen, not a single one is wearing a mask, including at the airport. I am not wearing a mask because I am immunocompromised and COVID could kill me like it has tried to twice already. I am wearing a mask because they need to witness someone who is wearing a mask, puncturing the fabric of their culture. I posted a video about collectivism and masking and within hours, a local organizer sent me a beautiful message saying that they realized I was correct— after some resistance— and were hoping to switch over several events to mask-encouraged events. It is not the destination, but that is the impact of a single person wearing a mask.

Liberation is in fact so easily achieved, if only we cared for it. Similarly, the eye makeup and fabulousness (as if I can ever not be fabulous) are to disrupt this culture where everyone is meant to look the same. It is the same white culture I encounter everywhere. My being is transformative, but it is not about creating a better life for myself, it is about community transformation for the person who yearns to wear makeup and dress fabulously and feels they can not. It is for the disabled immunocompromised person who is quarantining while everyone else pretends everything is fine. It is not fine.

Showing up in these capacities is not because I feel like I am a burden or I am not worthy. Perhaps, here and in my childhood, it was never about being a burden as in unworthy of care, rather I do not need care from those that are seemingly dying while providing care.

When I walked away to Saudi Arabia, it was not to perish. I walked away knowing that even as a two-year-old, I knew I would be fine. I no longer needed to witness Mama crying under the weight of four children, a newly dead mother, and displacement to a new country. I was tired even back then, and I knew alone I would be okay.

That never changed. I left, again and again. Until I left one day and never lived with them again. My relationship with my family is fraught right now. It is hard to be in one-sided and extractive relationships. They do not know better. I expect them to learn. Neither of us is willing to compromise. I do not compromise. Not because of them, but because in a world filled with genocide due to settler colonialism, imperialism, patriarchy, and capitalism, they are not very high on my care priority list. I support hundreds of people, who support hundreds of people. In the scale of community, they don't weigh very high.

A lot of feelings come up for me as I write all this. The first is feeling self-conscious, wondering how people will judge the last statement. That statement makes me sound harsh and callous. I don't actually care, for in a world where true callousness is celebrated while community care is seen as evil, I do not care for society's expectations much. However, there is a part of me that wishes things could be different. This part is filled with sorrow and longing, because my sisters could have been part of my community, and instead choose individualism. Some uncertainty and confusion are also coming up: Are we born collectivists? Can we learn it? Who did I learn it from?

I mean real liberatory collectivism. I don't mean a love for a single community or one's family. I mean collectivism. I mean that the humanity within me honors the humanity within you even as you're killing me.

Recipe for collectivism

1 part autism
1 part queerness
1 part transness
9 parts displacement
2 parts Palestine
1 part disability
1 part cancer moon
4 parts leo

I think I was raised collectivist. My family lost that part of themselves assimilating in Jordan. No matter how good a community is, if it's an assimilative collectivism it will never lead to liberation. Assimilative collectivism is in fact allyship individualism. People come together to create a whole in the face of an enemy. When the enemy is destroyed, the destruction turns inward.

Most organizing communities, from what I have witnessed across dozens of countries, are assimilative collectivism. It is why most pro-Palestinian spaces will not center me, feeling that my transness will fracture the trust they have built in the space. In this regard non-trans people, including queer people, believe that allyship with transphobes is more strategic than allyship with trans Palestinians ourselves, thinking that numbers will protect them. It is a basic survival instinct, and they are wrong. They are assimilating into a community that will tear itself apart as soon as the threat of external destruction is reduced. It has and is already happening.

Liberatory Collectivism is different.

Values of Liberatory Collectivism

1. Center the most marginalized always

Liberation is needed because systems of oppression create hierarchies and systems of violence that marginalize. The most marginalized of the most marginalized are always closest to liberation. It sounds like it would be the opposite, but we are not weighed down by the fallacy of privilege. We can not move towards power if we wanted to. This is why poor Disabled Global Majority trans community are some of the most liberated individuals out there. There are other even more marginalized groups, and they are closer still. This is not to say that everyone within the most marginalized groups is liberated. This is saying that we have more things that move us towards doing the internal work needed for liberation, and less enticement to avoid this work and avoid liberation.

2. Honor allyship but work to build comradery

A good friend often speaks about how allyship is about war and that they want everyone to be a comrade. I am in enthusiastic agreement with them on the first part, but I do not believe that everyone is ready for comradery with me. They are simply not ready. They have not done the work and have not earned the right to be my comrade. To die for someone is an immense honor, one that most people are not ready for. We work towards that.

I live a life built on faith. So when someone says they are in this, I will act like they are. What happens after does not matter. Comradery though, requires individuals to not feed off the things that are actively harming communities—mine and others. You can not be in denial about benefiting from genocide and be my comrade. You are an ally. You feed off my blood as we unite against a shared enemy. You harm me throughout and after. In the process, you either move towards comradery or we move towards making your harm irrelevant.

3. Transcend any one individual community

I don't put my life on the line for Palestinian community. It is never about one. A free Falasteen has the capacity to begin a chain reaction that transforms the world and ends settler colonialism. I support queer and trans folks and queer and trans Palestinians because I know of our transformative power. It is not actually about the queer and trans community, it's that there is no liberation without us. I care about people and at the end of the day, strategy is needed.

4. Transform conflict

Conflict is what allows the above to materialize and move. Conflict is momentum. We are hovering in free space, frozen until conflict propels us one way or another. Conflict is always helpful, even when it tears apart communities. We will not all be the right comrades for one another, we are not ready.

Conflict shines a light to the root cause of what attempts to rob us of our power, what marginalizes us. By addressing this root cause we transform conflict, propelling us forward to true comradery.

5. Alchemize growth towards liberation

Growth is always happening. Some honor it and allow it to guide them. Others push it down, doing all they can to glue themselves wherever they might be. Growth is just a reality, neither positive or negative. One can grow into facism or into liberation. Nothing is wasted; we alchemize every experience of growth and use it to move towards liberation.

6. Claim death

Death is prophesied for all of us. It will always occur. It is a blessing that will always occur, whether we want it or not. Claiming death allows us to see beyond marginalization. White supremacy and the other systems are drops in buckets in comparison to the expansiveness of humanity and beyond. Death claims everything, including systems of oppression and liberation, alchemizing everything into something.

7. Embrace limits and move beyond them

To be weak is to be malleable. Be weak in the face of an obstacle. If we do not embrace the limitations set for us we do not know how to move past them. This is why the most marginalized of the most marginalized must be centered. We know these limits intimately and violently and we move beyond them everyday. We do not have time to consider what is possible and what is not and we have nothing left to lose. That is what makes us terrifying in the face of systems of oppression. We are limitless. Community is limited when we assimilate into privilege. The limit of community is assimilation.

"The master's tools will not dismantle the master's house." Audre Lorde

How would we build the very thing that will end the master's house by listening to the limits set by the master?

We deserve liberation. Liberation does not happen on a large scale without collectivism. Individual liberation is just another word for assimilation.

Community Care as Practice

Community Care as Practice

A version of this essay was first published in UHURU: Liberation Planner by organized by avé 鳥

When they come for you, who will be there? Who will support you?

We talk about the zombie apocalypse and who we need around. We think of practical skills, who can gather food, who can hunt, who can build things with their hands, who can shoot arrows or whatever else. Maybe who can fish, who can grow food, who can birth children. But we talk about zombies, not realizing that the zombies are the government, and the skills above are inadequate.

They come for us, when we are visible and when we are invisible. Arguably, we are more protected when we are visible, yet the fall still happens.
Imperialism is basic, using the same set of tools, again and again, nearly perfected in its machine. We were told to be cogs in this machine, yet most still can't even name the machine, let alone the different parts of it. I think we're scared to name things, because even those of us who know the system intimately are

shamed out of talking about it because we don't always have the right words. Even when we do, academia tells us we don't know what we're talking about, but we have always known our oppressors, even as their hands are squeezing our necks, we know them. We have always known them.

Years ago, I joked that they took our land because we welcomed them into our homes for three days before we asked them why they were there. I felt like our kindness was abused. It was. And maybe our kindness makes us vulnerable. It does.

The above implies that we were passive in our colonization; the reality is that we resisted, we fought back, and they massacred us with British weapons. We saw them tightening their arms around our necks, and yes, we resisted, we will always resist, but when tasked with using their own weapons against them, we refused then and refuse now.

My people have experienced genocide again and again. Genocided by different groups of people, almost always white. Yet, we do not wish the same on anyone and never have. So, what makes a people crave genocide? What makes them actually go through with it? What makes them savor it? I ask for any of you who sit by as people are genocided, as group after group—often concurrently—are.

And what makes a community of care?

I learned community care from my family post the Gulf War. I am not sure if my parents knew community care before they packed a car and drove across a desert months before I was born. Maybe they learned it from their own childhoods, fleeing a different war, past the same desert to Kuwait from Palestine in the '60s. Maybe it was already in their bones when their parents carried their things and fled in 1948, maybe it was before that as the British butchered entire families. Maybe it was the migration. Maybe...
I was born knowing community care, not because it was cute but because we needed it to survive.
We survived. In Jordan. In Arizona.
We didn't bring community care to Arizona, it was already there.
We were dropped off at the Islamic Cultural Center in Tempe. Baba's best friend's family lived in LA. We flew to them first, they drove us across the desert.

It was Ramadan, Taraweeh prayer in the background. They didn't know we were coming, but we were there.

Baba talked to Amo, Mama was introduced to the babysitter who took care of all the kids downstairs. There was movement. They put us in a one-bedroom motel. One night. Two nights. Three. They found us a place. They showed us how to grocery shop. They took us to the park for a picnic where the white woman released her dogs on us, but that's a different story. There are many stories of how I learned cruelty. They helped Baba get a full-time restaurant job. Mama started tutoring kids and adults in Arabic, babysitting left and right. We walked to school the next Monday, across train tracks in grey, both the checkered suit I wore on my first day and the sky that normally would have been blue. Someone drove us back, Mama took care of their kids, fed them. They gave us furniture and clothes and the one stuffed animal I had pre-the age of 24. We took care of one another in my community.

I learned community care because otherwise we would not have survived.

This is the community care I learned about (it was rarely branded with these words, but the concepts have always been a part of everything I knew and know now) :

1) Ta'awun تعاون, Tabadul تبدل
Ta'awun: collaboration
Tabadul: mutual assistance

We offer what we can, no judgements, no questions, we just do. It will look different for everyone and every offering is a gift. There is nothing wasted.
Let's be honest, childcare, transportation, and meals are essential. Yet, often it is money that is seen as the most valuable. Everyone I grew up with reminds me how my home growing up was the place they came to for a home-cooked meal and family, in a way they did not have elsewhere. My house was their home. We may have been the most financially impoverished for a little while, but our house was as rich as a seven layer chocolate cake. I remember the food that seemed to appear from nowhere even when we could not afford any trips to Chuck E. Cheese.

2) Takaful تكافل
Takaful: tying survival together, putting yourself on the line, as if you had bailed someone out

Takaful is an Arabic term derived from the root word 'Kafala' or 'Takafala' which means to guarantee or to mutually guarantee.

We do not choose who we are in community with. Our community are those whose survival is tied to ours and who are showing up for us.

We moved to a community in Arizona filled with all kinds of people and the first people we were in community with were SWANA folks, but the ones who we were truly in community with were Black Americans. As the SWANA folks assimilated into privilege, it was half a dozen years of my family in community with Black, not SWANA families. I will not pretend as if my parents had dealt with their own anti-Blackness: my dad with his family's internalized anti-Blackness, constantly trying to move away from their Sudanese heritage, and Mama's side holding onto their lighter skinned privilege that the British elites loved. Mama wouldn't do this work until after we left Arizona. However, according to the Black people I grew up with, she was the only Arab who was safe. When we have to show up we show up, there is nothing that can stop us when our survival is tied and we show up for one another.

3) Mawadah مودة
Mawadah: a kindness that extends beyond actions or words derived from the root of fondness and love.

The English definition of love is nowhere near enough for what the word Mawadah means. Where love implies a conscious connection, Mawadah is something deeply rooted in spirit that can not falter. If love is a verb, Mawadah is the value system that allows it to exist, it is the root of love, affection, kindness.

We carry one another towards liberation, or no one is carried at all. Assimilation is the opposite of carrying and support one another towards liberation. Assimilation is the guise of personal liberation. You may pretend that assimilation is liberation, but assimilation has never liberated anyone.

4) Niza3 نزاع, Nidal نضال, Tasamuh تسامح

Niza3: Struggle that's built on carrying with one another, conflict

**Nidal: is a struggle that you champion.
Tasamuh: Forgiveness**

Disposability is not an option.

Mama got into one large fight with Khalto A. I don't remember what she did, or who was to blame, but they stopped talking. The thing though, is that they weren't in community together, letting go of one another had zero consequences. There were other fights, other things that came up, they were either dealt with, or they did not matter enough. When you were community, you were not disposable. Even when harm was caused, separation happened but accountability was always the way to move back into community. We needed one another, and it's in that vulnerability that we were everything.

What is forgiveness when disposability is not an option?

We are taught we must forgive to move past and if we do not it is a never-ending conflict. But what does that mean in a community where not working together is an easily accessible choice?

I was canceled in 2018 by two of the most violent individuals I have ever come across. One abused me for 18 months before a suicide attempt led me into three hospitals and 18 months of houselessness. This person jeopardized my immigration process, nearly getting me deported. They have gotten others deported, others evicted, others into mental health hospitals. The trail of destruction of young adults is truly remarkable.

Yet when this person reached out to community partners, instead of folks actually having a conversation, it was treated as a "believe brown cis-women against everyone else" situation, which is TERFy (Trans Exclusionary Radical Feminist) and TMERFy (Trans Masculine Exclusionary Radical Feminist) and always harms trans people.

Despite the harm this has caused, if any of these individuals are at the forefront of work that is essential for my communities' liberation, I would work with them. I don't have to like them or forgive them. I will do what I can to make the power that allows them to harm individuals irrelevant but beyond that, they're not significant enough in my world to warrant the need for forgiveness and rebuilding relationships. Unfortunately, not a single one of these individuals is actually involved in intersectional liberation work. They are still TERFs and TMERFs, actively gate keeping trans people out of movements and continuing to cause harm to the most marginalized within the community. If they were to move past that, then we can work together.

5) Hanaa هناء

Hanaa: joy and wellness, the root of everything happy

We do more than survive, we dance in joy between the ruins that genocide leaves behind.

As a child, they took us to the grand canyon. They took us fishing. They took us to a gift shop and there is a picture of us. I got a Sega and a Simba. We got Barbies and Disney movies. There was so much more than survival.

None of us are well if any of us are not well.

When one member is not well it has a domino effect.
When one member is well it has a domino effect.
There is no denying that in relationship, we are always one.

For some reason the word Hanaa is, for me, connected to the concept of bathing. Probably because my uncle is named Naeem and my mom is named Hanaa. We say Naeeman when you take a shower or after a haircut. It's hard to define, but it can be connected to "blessings" or "comfort."

When I think of showers and baths, I think about the act of cleansing. The act of allowing something to release and then cleanse. How does happiness cleanse our souls? Or is it that we cleanse our souls and find happiness? Both?

In the spring of 2023, during an eclipse week I wrote this poem during a retreat:

Gratitude

Is inseparable from
Forgiveness

In Arabic
"You're welcome"
Meaning forgiving
A releasing or acquaintance
Of guilt and pain

I forgive through gratitude, you
Forgive through ...

Forgiveness عفو
Is also rooted in عافية
Healing,
Wellness, whatever
Inadequate english words to say:
Gratitude is
Forgiveness is
Healing is
Wellness is
Wholeness is
Me

6) Tama3un تمعّن, Tafakkur تفكر, Tadabbur تدبر, Tadhakkur تذكر

Tama3un: concentration, Tafakkur: contemplation, Tadabbur: reflection,

Tadhakkur: rememberance

We notice, we witness, we show up when asked and when we are not asked.

You do not walk into a Palestinian household without a gift, not if you're Palestinian. You do not walk into another's house without a gift, not if you're Palestinian. In a practice of community care we witness and then we gift when we are able to. The number of times that someone walked into our home with exactly the right thing and vice versa.

Recently, a friend told another friend that she used to skateboard and within twelve hours a skateboard was provided.

Reflection is not only an internal process. A mirror does not hide what it sees. A mirror reflects back what it witnesses. Within capitalist spirituality folks will meditate and commit genocide in between their breaths. Reflection does not make you a better person. How you show up is what makes you a good person.

7) Karam كرم

Karam: generosity

We ask for support. We receive support. We gift support.

Being ashamed of receiving support is white supremacy and capitalism telling us we must do it on our own otherwise we have failed.

"How do you expect to be part of the solution if you can't ask for help?" I don't remember who I said this to, but they're welcome. The best community care practitioners are those of us who have needed care to survive. We are past the capitalist shame about accepting support. We ask for support, we receive support and we gift support back to our community. None of us can do this alone, and an unwillingness to accept support is just white supremacy and capitalism.

8) Tatawur تطور, Tawasu3 توسع

Tatawur: evolution

Tawasu3: expansion

We grow. If you are not growing, something is very wrong in your community. We grow. We develop. We evolve. We expand in everything we are.

Our contributions change over time as our relationship with privilege changes.

Baba graduated in 2003, and for a year he had an engineer's salary in Arizona. Now we were the ones who could show up with financial support rather than be on the receiving end. We pivoted, still always showing up for community.

9) Waajib واجب

Waajib: responsibility/duty

In Islam, it means something that is mandatory like mandatory prayers, fasting, etc.

Everyone has a role to play.

I was grocery shopping at the age of 7, carrying my weight in bags, making decisions, sometimes wrong ones. One time I was asked if we needed bread and we hadn't bought any in a while. I said yes but didn't have enough money, so Amo said I could pay it next time. I carried the twenty pound box of pita bread to the car and Mama yelled at me because we didn't actually need it. Baba had bought some, but Baba never bought pita, it was always me. I made the wrong decision once about potatoes, and I made hundreds of right decisions. I hold onto these wrongs, because in a way they helped me understand my responsibilities. Before I knew multiplication tables I knew how to keep track of money for groceries. Buying potatoes at the wrong time meant we had no money for some other things. Buying extra pita meant our freezer did not have space.

No child should have to do this labor, but also no child should ever experience genocide, displacement, food and housing insecurity, and everything else that my people have experienced for generations due to settler colonialism.

The circumstances in my life that allowed me to begin practicing community care are not things I would wish on anyone. We do need violence to learn responsibility and to learn community care. Knowing and experiencing community care is what allowed me to survive the adversity, it was not adversity that taught me how to care for my community.

I will always practice community care because my people have only ever known community care.

10) Sumud صمود

Sumud: A steadfastness and resolve that transcends the possibility of ever being destroyed

In one of the most well known Quran Chapters "Al-Ikhlas," Allah says "ٱللَّهُ ٱلصَّمَدُ" which translates to "Allah—the Sustainer" or "Allah—the Absolute". In other spaces it is defined as "the Eternal."

Since October 7th, 2023, there is more cognition about the Palestinian value of Sumud. It is a value beyond the English capabilities to define it. If you google "eternal resolve" you get a music album, these words incomprehensible together. Yet our entire existence is about Sumud.

To me Sumud is about Utopia. In the face of immense injustice what do we do? "Stand up, fight back," always. I wonder if the people who say this phrase know what it actually means. It means that when we're tired we stand up and fight back. It means when we are happy and joyful we stand up and fight back. It means our rest is standing up and fighting back. It means that to our core we are never well if we do not stand up and fight back.

For years, I saw my grandfather looking off into the distance mid-conversation at times, or in his garden where he spent the majority of the last 15 years of his life. He looked off, towards Palestine, towards home. He grew the trees of his childhood, and in a 20-sq-ft garden created his own possibility of Utopia, but he never stopped looking off into the distance, towards his true home, where his house remains but is settled by zionist settlers in the settler-colonial state of Israel. He died December, 2020 due to heart failure and COVID-19, at the age of 89, two weeks before his 90th birthday. He died in Salt, Jordan, a city that used to be a gateway between Palestine and Jordan, back when settler colonialism hadn't taken home away.

Like many others from Palestine, I have found myself rushing to the Mediterranean Sea any time I can. As the salty water bathes my skin it almost feels like I'm on the beaches of Yaffa, my ancestral home. I look to the southeast often when I am there, yearning for the home that I have keys for, but no way of returning to.

Yet, every day, I dream. I dream, my sisters dream, my grandfather dreamed, and millions of Palestinians dream of the day when we may return home, and when the constant void and heartbreak end. Of course, there's no way of knowing if those two will end, but we have faith and allow that faith to spirit our hope.

Sumud does not exist without faith. Faith is about transcendence. You can not have collectivism without faith and spirituality. If it's not obvious, spirituality is not religion. Spirituality can never be defined as a single practice. Spirituality transcends any boundaries and binds we place upon ourselves.

None of these values stand alone. They intersect like a spiral, constantly elevating one another and if one is missing, the spiral is just lines hovering in space, aimless, directionless, powerless.

On Strategy

On Strategy

I have been facilitating political education sessions for nearly 15 years. Yet, today in June 2024 is the first time that I've run a building strategy session.

It is not that I haven't discussed strategy in the hundreds of other sessions that I have had. I discuss strategy all the time. However, the gap that I am noticing is a conversation about what is strategy instead of what is strategic.

Today's session was intended to focus on something other than strategy. This session is a Building Utopia workshop, but during my week in Norway—talking to organizers and through questions from other events—it's become apparent that breaking down strategy is essential.

Even this session does not fully serve as a strategy building session. We still focus on the practical ways to enact strategy, not necessarily developing it or more accurately, but developing the skillset.

Strategy is defined as: a plan of action designed to achieve a long-term or overall aim.

The concept predates the word, being coined to signify generals in armies. Strategy is survival, we have always survived.

We have always had to be strategic.

When I left home to try to save my family from death (thank you psychosis) I negotiated every day who I could be around, which impacted where I slept that evening, if at all. Very quickly, my strategy became to spend a minimal amount of time around anyone. I thought that it was the duration of time spent with others that led to the individuals around me dropping dead. It meant if I had lunch with someone, I slept on a park bench. If I had no contact I could sleep on a friend's couch, and so on and so forth. That became my strategy. Being on the border of Syria as the Syrian revolution began meant this strategy did not prevent loved ones from being killed, but it satisfied my psychosis. This was the short term, the long term and end goal being that I would be dead.

In November 2010, a part of my brain asked "what happens if we don't die?" It was a 2% chance, and due to this percentage I had to rethink strategy.

Suddenly, the strategy became that I needed care. Care was not available at the border of war. So, I searched for care. I looked at Lebanon first, I was not pleased. I should have looked at Europe but I did not know Europe. The US felt more accessible. So, how does an unhoused person who graduated high school with 69%—in a country that would not have accepted me into any engineering or even science programs—end up in an engineering school with a 4.0-GPA-acceptance rate? (I take a sip of coffee). Well, it's because the admissions officer met me.

It was raining that day, I was visiting my family and, as always, in my attempt to avoid them so they don't self-combust, I went to an admissions session that was meant to make US and UK universities more accessible for those of us who were not in 20K-JOD-a-year-private schools (strange when the university has a $65K USD tuition a year, but whatever). There was no one else, most likely due to the rain. I don't remember our conversation, but I knew that if I applied I would be getting in, despite the low grades. The bigger question was scholarship. As an international student, financial aid is rarely available for us.

Here's where the decision-making comes in. I may have known I would get accepted but the application fee was $65 or some number near there, making January a light food month. However, the $500 deposit was another story altogether. The choice was between no food for three months as war rages in Syria to the north or submit this deposit and then figure out how I'm going to get another $1000 for a flight and $10,000 for my first semester. Once there, I knew I could get multiple jobs and be fine, it was the before that concerned me. I made the deposit.

The following three months would be the worst physically in my life. By the end of those three months I had lost 45lbs, down to 120lbs. This is after a year where bones would break, where I would pass out at least once a day, after... (there are too many instances to list). It was a difficult time, and it was the best thing for me at the time.

I talked to Baba after my visa was approved that summer. He said he would book my flight. Seedo (Baba's dad) randomly decided that he was going to split his kids' inheritance that summer. My dad received the exact amount I needed for that first semester, so he loaned it to me.

Mama was livid with Baba for "allowing" this to happen. I landed in Boston without knowing how to get to campus. I used a pay phone, figured it out, made it to campus to an empty dorm room with no sheets and no bedding, things I thought would be there.

I was the first person hired at the call center that year. I became a tour guide. I became a Resident Advisor. I started working for the career development office. I had internship after internship. I did a co-op at an engineering company my sophomore year. I did everything I could. I worked across countries, and every penny went to a school that funnels engineers and scientists to arms dealers and the sustainers of genocide.

After, I worked at one of the most sought after roles in one of the few non-arms dealing Fortune 500 companies. I co-founded a nonprofit with a group of primarily early twenties. We were led by one of the most vile individuals I have ever come across; most of the young board was destroyed by a woman in her mid-40s.

I started my own non-profit as that was happening. I began facilitating peer support certification training. I applied for an EB 2 visa, watching my chances dwindle as Trump got elected. Watching my application be delayed by 8 months because of the person mentioned above.

My therapist told me to leave, get in my car and leave. After three hospitals and losing parts of my soul. That sounds cliche, as if we can ever lose parts of ourselves, but just like our cells regenerate every 7 years our soul endlessly generates and regenerates. We leave parts of us everywhere we are, and sometimes people forcibly take pieces of us, cannibalizing them.

I drove away, to every continental state in what's known as the United States. I found some of those pieces along the way, those pieces and other pieces lost over decades of violence. We do not need to map the same journey of loss to find the pieces. I found the pieces lost to Jordan at the age of 4, in Colorado. I found the pieces of being 21 in Arizona—the pieces of growing up in Arizona—in the Nevada Desert. I found pieces I didn't know were lost, in the South. I wrote a book in the process, or rather, finished a book that was started on a rooftop in Vietnam months earlier.

Life has an interesting way of making itself known, of finding the unhealed cycles and tearing them to shreds until we find the magic just beyond them.

Strategy in my life has never been about a single plan, it is 17 plans converging at the exact moments that they need to. Strategy is honoring the millions of factors we can't control and composing a symphony within those factors to move beyond them. We are composers, yet we have not invented music as a whole. To move one step at a time is a privilege and luxury we do not have.

It is the same with worldbuilding. Utopia, liberation, justice, etc. will not happen with a single course of action, a single plan. Liberation happens when we have spread so many seeds of love and light in every direction—allowing them to grow and thrive beyond anything we can feel or witness—that they converge in perfect harmony, systems of oppression shattering on contact. We do not know when this moment will come, but we know it will.

I want to go back to being 13. I am in English class or math class, I am sketching. Home is violent, because Canada's refugee systems are violent, so every day Mama, Baba, and I are in a screaming match about going back to Jordan. I am exhausted, and I decide to leave.

It would have been easy to just leave. Instead, I decided to write a novel because J.K. Rowling is not better than me and even she can make a billion dollars. I write every day in classes, because I was going to be financially independent. I would visit Mama, and only Mama, maybe the babies, but I wasn't fully thinking of them until I took N out in a blizzard and decided they would come with me or I would care for them distantly.

I had to write a book, graduate, find an agent, get a publisher, get emancipated, and fly and move to NYC. These sound like they would happen in order, instead they had to happen all at once. The book would be done by the time agents responded asking for it, the court filing would be filed by then, the only thing that would wait is the flight, because I needed the advance. It was this preparedness that allowed me to pivot and force my family to move to Jordan so Mama can be with her dad when he dies.

Strategy is never wasted, even when it doesn't lead us where we thought it might.

I am grateful that my life has never allowed me to approach strategy with a single-issue mindset. At the margins, life is never a single issue.

As I write this, I am in Norway. Norway has finally recognized Palestine as a real place. In the media, Norway is seen as a sort of Utopia that honors everyone, where everyone is rich and there is no racism of any kind. In reality, Norway is as racist as any other white place and still despises Palestinians. To come to Norway I needed to apply for a visa. I applied well in advance to come from June 20th to July 1st to speak and host workshops during Pride week. The ask was simple and very concrete, I was invited by Oslo Pride. Yet, my Jordanian passport does not arrive back from the Norwegian embassy until July 1st. If my US passport had not come in early I would not have been in Norway. Plans are constantly converging on one another, thousands at a time.

Strategy is being able to witness the web, predict what's to come and act—again and again.

So, what does that mean?

Witness

There are 15 people in the coffee shop I am sitting in, mostly brown people. They speak a mix of Hindi, Urdu, Arabic, English, and Norwegian. Some stare at me, but most don't energetically interact with me. I'm in the Black and Brown part of town, where white Norwegians are uneasy. Some people have children. This is the day after Pride. There is a spike in COVID-19 rates. It is about to rain. There is a slightly cold breeze coming in through the door I am beside.

Predict

The COVID-19 rate will rise in the coming week as all the Pride COVID hits. This new variant will hit them hard, the variant "FLiRT" making itself undeniable. Going through Manchester airport I am livid that not a single person is wearing a mask. I am livid but I am not surprised. I was surprised by Oslo, expecting at least one mask, I am wrong. Belfast I am not surprised by at all.

We can predict that people will not be masking and in fact, people in general will not keep us safe, we will keep us safe. The "We" here is complex to say the least: who in fact is actually keeping us safe, when folks are trying to protect one of our identities while killing us for another? We witness things and recognize the patterns of how others will show up. Unfortunately, it is not very complex. Most of this is predictable.

Act

I don't normally neti pot every day if I am not traveling, but I do these days. I use a nasal spray, I mask, and I test routinely. I take immunity supplements, my diet is designed to prevent me getting sick. I also do not go around unsafe people, or go around people more immunocompromised than I am if I might have been impacted. It's difficult to prevent this entirely, but we can act in one, two, three ways and so much more.

Let's go a level deeper

Witness

London Breed, San Francisco's mayor at the time this was written, has been working to criminalize homelessness. Elon Musk has been on a similar campaign to talk about how "unsafe" San Francisco has become. The masses agree, including marginalized communities—primarily middle class and upper middle class communities—and others who are barely surviving within capitalism as well.

We witness.

The pro-Palestine movement post October 7th, 2023, like BLM before it, unleashes chaos that is undeniable. Masses are protesting. Masses are masked.

We witness.

Predict

Legislative sessions follow a yearly calendar. Holidays and months supposedly for the most marginalized serve as reminders for when they come after us (at least a little more). It is easy to predict that in May and June anti-trans sentiment will rise, it has for years now to ensure that we are able to "celebrate" Pride. This will always happen. The Supreme Court is also easy to predict, always making decisions when folks are distracted. Distraction is a favorite tool of the system. Last week, the last week of Pride 2024, the supreme court decided to support criminalizing houselessness, immunity for presidents, and overturning Chevron v. Natural Resources Defense Council.

It's easy to predict fascism. Too easy.

Act

It's easy to act when you know what the system is, when you are able to predict the system after witnessing it. So we act.

The state criminalizes homelessness. We divest from the state and build our own housing structures.

The state criminalizes mutual aid. We build jobs that allow individuals to move past capitalism and work to destroy it.

The state criminalizes our existence. We move underground.

We move underground.

We move underground.

Out of these essays, this is the only exhausting one to write. It's exhausting because we do not have time to really develop this skillset, not when we're running around endlessly. Not when we are fighting dozens of things all at the same time, our brains going a million miles a minute. Not when it feels like most people still are not seeing the dozens of things, or don't care to see the dozens of things, and in the time it takes to teach about one area, we are fully depleted. Communities built on extraction.

Yet, this is where strategy is needed most. Strategy is not about doing the things that are easy. Strategy is needed most when moving forward seems impossible. Strategy is also not finding the one thing. Being strategic requires us to know that we must try dozens of things along the way. We act, again and again.

Part of my strategy is supporting individuals to be able to connect the dots in building a foundation that allows them to act whether or not they truly understand the interconnections.

I don't believe we have a political education problem, I believe we have an individualism problem that allows people to believe that they need to understand everything before taking action. You will never understand me, not unless we live the same life. I will never understand what it's truly like to be a dark-skinned Black person. I don't need to. What I need to know how to do is to honor people, step back, use my privilege, and act again and again, recognizing that my life and other people's lives are on the line. Those are the skillsets I aim to develop in my fellowship programs, my trainings, my writing, my speaking, everything.

When They Come for Us

When They Come for Us

I received my US passport hours after being told the FBI was asking about me, and something told me they weren't asking about me like you did in 7th grade to see if someone likes you. I've made my feelings pretty clear and so did they. Sometimes we're just not meant to be.

I'm not going to lie, I was stressed, not necessarily because they were asking about me. I expect them to be reading these very words before they're published. I was stressed because I have seen their intimidation tactics work so successfully.

I was nine when they came to our house in Tempe, Arizona post-9/11. Some bullshit about one of the hijackers living next door to us, a narrative they used again and again. I felt the fear in that room, not because Mama knew anything about this person who supposedly was our neighbor, but because we know the difference between one kind of police state and another, is visibility.

What's known as the US has always been a police state, an oligarchy, and authoritarian in all ways except for the public branding. Post-9/11, folks were deported, citizenships revoked, folks disappearing to black sites and Guantanamo Bay. Folks simply disappeared.

I watched it happen, my nine-year-old eyes watching, listening, witnessing as it happened. I understood it because Mama understood it; in many ways I have always been the part of Mama that processes and remembers. They disappeared and were met with silence, years before social media would allow us to talk about state violence on a large platform. Even now, you could disappear, a drop in a bucket of state-organized disappearances.

9/11 destroyed Muslim organizing almost entirely. One day changed it all. But it wasn't one day. It was two decades earlier that the Zionist state tried to brand Palestinians as terrorists. It was two decades of policy being launched little by little. It was two decades of Hollywood deforming us little by little.

By 9/11 there was nothing left. 9/11 did not create Islamophobia. 9/11 cemented protections for the state that allowed it to label anyone as a terrorist if they disagreed or showed opposition. 9/11 allowed white supremacy to fissure Global Majority populations while harming them all, taking away attention from Black and Indigenous folks and instead focusing on Muslims and more broadly immigrants. Within whiteness, there is no difference between Muslims and immigrants, not because we all look the same, but because dehumanizing groups of people as other hated people is part of their violence. Often immigrants are racialized as Muslims and Muslims are racialized as immigrants.

This shift has only harmed Black and Indigenous communities, supposedly ushering an age beyond race in the fight against racism. One needs to only look at Black media pre and post the 9/11 era to notice this shift. Throughout the '80s and '90s, there was a wealth of nearly entirely Black cast shows, such as In Living Color, Living Single, and so many more. In the early 2010s we had Blackish.

This shift was felt everywhere—in different ways. 9/11 changed the trajectory of the second Intifada, leading to the 2006 Zionist state war with Lebanon.

I'd imagine that many have talked about the cultural impacts of 9/11 globally, and that the main takeaway is that whiteness was the only beneficiary of 9/11.

9/11 was 23 years ago today (written on 9/11/2024). An entire generation has never known a world before. Since then, we have experienced COVID, and we have seen the Occupy, BLM, #Metoo, and Palestine liberation movements rise.

It is ethically undeniable how much Global Majority communities have benefited from the BLM movement. It is also ethically undeniable that we (the non-Black community) have failed the Black community time and again, including during the height of BLM.

At the height of BLM, as white folks were grappling with a post-Black Beyonce world and as Brown people were immediately elevated yet again as "proof" of a post-racial world, BLM organizers were disappeared, assassinated, kidnapped, and trafficked into prisons.

Black and Indigenous folks have been telling us all along. Other Global Majority folks have been telling us. Trans folks have been telling us. Disabled folks have been telling us. Very few folks have not been telling the world. Yet, very few folks have been listening, actually listening. Our communities' separation did not start on 9/11. Separation has been built into settler colonialism and imperialism from day one. 9/11 was just another...I don't even have a word for it. Another tool? Another weapon? Another word? Another reminder? 9/11 was another one of those.

October 7th, 2023 was another.

They came for us then. They are coming for us now. They are always coming for us.

We are not prepared.

The tenets of fascism include authoritarianism supported by a police and military state, nationalism, and some kind of hierarchy. White Christian nationalism covers the last two. Authoritarianism is a little trickier, requiring control of the judicial, executive, and financial systems of a state. Experts who have researched this for decades longer than I have can speak intimately about these factors.

What matters to me is a recognition that with a white Christian Nationalist supreme court, a white Christian Nationalist executive government, and white Christian Nationalist funding structures, what is left? What's left is not a Democratic president in office. What's left is a full move to authoritarian policy and an expansion of the police state.

If you're not paying attention to cop cities, you need to be. Cop cities are the literal embodiment of occupying Black and Brown neighborhoods, expanding policing everywhere, and increasing the ability to deploy police with even more ease. This should terrify you.

The second part is the law. For decades we have watched right-wing states passing anti-abortion and anti-trans bills only to be deflected due to the existence of Roe v. Wade.

However, something a lot of us have been talking about the entire time is that just because a law is prevented on a federal level does not mean the law does not exist, it only means it is not enforceable. For example, the state of Alabama still has school segregation as part of its constitution. It can not enforce it *until* Brown v. Board of Education is overturned.

No law that passes is wasted, it is in waiting. Now, we are waiting, a minefield of policies and laws scattered around us, waiting.

So how'd we get here?

We are decades into multi-billion dollar campaigns that took something that was always evil (white supremacist imperialism) and used it to create barriers against any movement that rises against it.

There are the common tools we often discuss, such as purple, green, pink, red, and other rainbow colors of washing; and the weaponization of "civilization" to further the colonial project. There are the deeper global financial and governing tools of neo-liberalism, disguised as a post-racial form of democratic liberalism. Let's be honest, Clinton, Obama, and Biden have only benefitted fascism. One of the first things Biden did when he got into office was issue a domestic terrorism advisory that equated pro-life and pro-abortion organizers as the same. Obama created the foundation for many of the things Trump did in office (Muslim ban, drone program, border policies, and many others). The difference between the political parties in what's known as the US is visible and invisible pushes for fascism. This is one of the most critical things to remember, the lesser of two evils is a myth created to disrupt movements and separate our people.

The second enormous lie is that the white Christian nationalists are uneducated, unorganized, uncoordinated, and un- a lot of things. The reality is that the leaders of white Christian nationalism are the people who developed areas of academic studies, and they don't need to be perfectly organized and coordinated. Throw a billion dollars into a project and it will be somewhat effective. Our oppression doesn't need to be perfect.

We have to be efficient and effective because to their billion dollars, we have $100,000. For every policy they have to fall back on, we have a police officer's knee on our necks. For every dollar we fundraise for community care, we have FBI intimidation forcing our care work underground. They have billions, the CIA, FBI, the UN, the EU, nearly every international agency, hundreds of years of infrastructure, the police, and almost every politician. We have a community infested with infiltrators worldwide. Yeah, we have to be efficient and effective, our survival is dependent on it. On the other hand, the greatest threat to their survival is themselves.

Unfortunately, the greatest threat to our survival is also us, but always through them. Counterintelligence programs within Empire have always targeted movement leaders and community members to wreak havoc amongst our own. In turn, we are told that speaking publicly puts our people at risk. Every day I am told the genocide is my fault as a trans person because trans people need to be saved and at the same time my fault because I'm somehow also an FBI infiltrator leading to my people's genocide due to community violence.

They have power over us in the shadows. Today, it does not matter if a community member is an infiltrator or not, for the consequences are often the same. State violence runs deep within our communities and our minds. We are born within this system and all require immense deconditioning to be able to be with one another outside of their shadows.

They will weaponize us against one another regardless. We can make their narratives irrelevant and powerless by having conversations that allow us to challenge one another and hold the complexity of life within settler colonialism. We are not the same, and they can only weaponize that against us when we are unwilling to accept it.

They will come for us, within and outside of our communities. They are already coming, they have been for centuries. Are you ready?

We Move Underground

We Move Underground

We move underground.

The three words above sat on this page for weeks, some of the first written, yet nothing was added until the book was finished and well into the editing process.

I hesitated to write the words that come after "we move underground" because it feels like it defeats the purpose. Organizing and mobilizing carry risks, they have always carried risks. The risk looks different within a fascist state. The balance between visible and invisible work has always been necessary.

On the surface, within the community I grew up in, that balance shifted drastically post-9/11. Our ability to visibly protest changed. Our ability to have public conversations about our liberation changed. The FBI were in every one of our spaces. The FBI came into our homes. Only very small clusters of people would talk about anything. Everyone new to the community was seen as a possible infiltrator, creating restrictive trust-based practices for individuals to meet, or rather, to never meet.

Organizing continued, in smaller conversations, until my family left three years later. These were the years when any organizing was confined to private households and even the children were not aware of the conversations, but I have never been a child. These conversations were limited, purely an outlet to talk about liberation, not to create a liberated world.

I grew up in a very diverse community, but there was no more diversity. The politics of trust limit who we allow within our inner circles. Organizing went from a mix of Black Americans, Black immigrants, and people of SWANA, South Asian, and Eastern European descent to only Palestinian overnight. The work stopped being intersectional. The work eventually stopped entirely.

When the white supremacists started hosting weaponized rallies in the hundreds in front of the mosque I grew up in, there was very little organizing left. Then, a new generation of organizers rose. Today, I am not as familiar with the organizing happening in my old community, but the struggle and work continue.

Perhaps I struggled with writing this essay because I was initially intending to supply some pathways for underground organizing. Instead, it appears I need to discuss some of the things we leave behind when we move underground.

It's important to understand that when we say underground, we're not always talking about things that are prohibited, whether legally or culturally. The differences between things that are illegal through the law and those deemed illegal culturally are interesting. The law is not all-expansive, and in fact many of the things we deem as illegal are in fact legal. Very few people recognize that community care is illegal in many places. Many recognize that setting a building on fire is illegal, many will not recognize that giving someone food can be a greater legal offense.

Direct actions that require breaking the unequitable laws of colonizer and settler colonies are always underground. You do not plan on shutting down a bridge through public meetings. The do-not-disturb-the-peace part of the police's job is not kind to disturbing the peace of capitalism.

It's also important to understand that underground organizing is always happening all around us, whether the work is invisible due to legal necessity or to efficiency. Some things are easier done without the publicity.

Risk Assessment

We have always been underground. Underground for the direct actions that are seen as illegal. Underground for the actions that "disturb the peace" because they disturb capitalism. Underground because identities are racialized as terrorist regardless of what we organize. Underground because of shadow banning forcing us to post selfies to allow us to talk about genocide.

We have been underground. In every movement and in every cause for justice. It's important to understand what needs to move where and when, and when to risk more. Understanding community politics and governmental politics is critical. If you are not in community with people who understand the law, and policies, and who can strategically identify where these things are headed then you are not able to assess risk adequately. To organize without understanding risk is irresponsible and you can put a lot of people in harm's way in the process.

Understanding risk allows us to take risks. This is risky work and strategy requires us to take risks. If I know that doing community care work can get me arrested and no one around me knows this is a reality, me getting arrested could be a tool I use to get the word out. Risking arrest on camera is different than risking arrest in private where no one will witness the police brutality that is constant.

We must understand risk.

Reframing Trust

Due to the different risk levels, trust is often integral to underground organizing. However, it is not just a matter of trusting and doing this work with the right individuals, it also includes notions of culture of transparency and how it works within an ecosystem.

In many fundraising mutual aid practices individuals are conditioned to believe that transparency means seeing exactly where the money goes. This is dangerous when mutual aid has to move underground. When your standard of transparency is putting me or the people I work with at risk, we have defeated the purpose. This is why I do not share stories or images of the beneficiaries of mutual aid, even if safety permits. People know I do this work, but if they do not have faith in community taking care of community, then I do not have time for them to be a part of the work and toxifying the culture of care. Community care is one of the most criminalized areas of organizing and it is the area that people expect the most information from in exchange for material support. Community support includes providing food, funds, housing, and other forms of support. In most states in what's known as the United States it is illegal to feed unhoused individuals or provide direct funds to individuals. The risk has always existed in providing community care.

This belief stems from a saviorism complex. Community care inherently can not be about saviorism. When you donate $100 to queer and trans Palestinians, if the expectation is somehow you will be the one to save someone's life then you're coming into community care from a supremacist standpoint. Instead, donating $100 and knowing that this is a part of community, you do your part and hold hope that others will do theirs. And only when we all show up for one another do we begin getting to a place where community care is widespread and we truly take care of one another.

Interconnected and independent pods and ecosystems

I initially started writing that you can't do underground organizing on your own, but my experience tells me that's actually not true. There may be times where you are doing work on your own and no one understands why or knows you're doing it.

Ideally, even underground organizing happens in community. In community, we can strategize together, move together, protect one another, lift together. Alone, the work is possible and is done. Some things are easier done alone, others are far easier in community. Either way, this work must be connected to other work. You can not be strategic without understanding the landscape that required the labor in the first place and having a shared vision for the world we're heading towards. A liberated world will not happen because of a single person's actions. A liberated world is created when we rise as a community.

Due to the risk, in my opinion, whether underground or not, it is important to create independent pods of work. No person should ever own an entire area of work that dies out if they are no longer able to do the work.

I learned to organize as an adult as the Syrian Revolution began. I learned that I had to organize in a way that assumed that we have no idea who will be alive at the end of the day and no guarantee that any resource will exist at all. In practical terms, this looks like splitting work where it is owned by multiple people. The labor is split. The only time labor is held by an individual is for very strategic and short-term purposes when we are unable to spread the work.

I am connected to dozens of organizing pods. They each carry a little bit from the work I do. If any one of the pods are compromised the rest of the work continues and I move the work impacted to an existing or new pod. If something happens to me today, the vast majority of the work I am doing continues. It's public knowledge that I have multiple funds at any time, one fully controlled by me and the rest are a mix of individuals, community, and organizations. Along the way one or more of those has been impacted and I have had to rebuild infrastructure to adapt. And even though things were impacted, they never stopped and they won't stop until the work pivots and I am no longer involved in creating and distributing community care funds.

Moving past ego

You are invisible underground. Your name will not be remembered. Your labor never acknowledged. The people you fight for may be the ones to destroy you, call you a traitor, say you're doing nothing. You are underground.

Within the context of the Global North, we are all conditioned from the day we are born to be individualistic in ways that feed our ego. Individualism has no place in organizing, whether underground or otherwise. We must define ourselves as part of a vision of liberation and community.

Not everyone is able to do this long term, and that's okay. There are so many approaches. We do not do underground organizing for fame and fortune or any kind of validation. We organize because we have to. When organizing is a privilege for you and the outcome of your organizing does not matter to you, then you are not the right person to create strategy and lead.

We organize because we refuse to allow systems of oppression to be the best there is out there, we refuse and rebuke the lesser evil; we and everyone else deserve so much more. AND I acknowledge that many will benefit from others' oppression as well as our collective liberation. We are not all the same. Pretending we are within organizing can be deadly.

Letting Go

Letting Go

The trees in the distance sway in the wind but all I feel is the humidity in Haifa—until I write these words and a beautiful breeze cools me during the mid-day August heat. I am unbothered by the heat; my family was born of this temperature and although it has gotten worse in the 76 years since their exile, my skin remembers.

The hives dotting my skin from scalp to toes are not of the weather, although I wish they were. Instead they are from 10 months of activation since October 7th, on the fabric of a body that has never not been activated.

Before October 7th, I used to wake up with hives when a loved one was about to die, whether it was my grandfather or bell hooks. Now, they dot my skin, my brownness concealing them from prying eyes. The loss of loved ones is constant so the hives live with me, only infuriating when mosquitos use the rest of me as feeding grounds.

I am tired, as are so many others.

I thought I would tap out by April, but the magic of comrades stepping in to support queer and trans Palestinian work has allowed me to still be here, deep into August and better than expected.

However, I know this is not forever. I have known this is not forever. I am aware of where my mental health is at and where I am heading.

When I organize during crisis I organize recognizing that today might be my last day, for whatever reason. I learned this witnessing the Syrian revolution and the rest of the Arab Spring. No life was ever guaranteed. No resources were ever stable. I took this knowledge into all my organizing and mobilizing. Nothing is stable during times like these and if I don't build my work around this reality then my impact will always be surface level and potentially lead to more harm than good.

For years I have held strategic planning and vision-building spaces for organizations and communities, particularly social justice spaces. It amazes me how few places recognize that their vision should be to make themselves obsolete. Ultimately, a successful movement means an end to injustice and systems of oppression. My work should be obsolete.

More than that, I recognize that I can not be the movement nor should I ever be. I am currently in Falasteen for the very first time and to honor this experience and be with my community, I have taken a step back from most of my other organizing duties. This step back is not felt almost at all by the spaces I am in because I have spent months ensuring that there is infrastructure that exists beyond me. On the other hand, most of the other organizers I know in other communities carry the weight of no organizing happening when they take a step back. We see this worldwide.

As I write this, I am also aware of dozens of conflicts within organizing spaces and a few nights ago, talking to a queer Palestinian living in Palestine, I reflected on how it is easier for people to step away when a conflict arises. It is easier to walk away in flames than consciously saying I need to modify my work to allow me to continue to be here for years to come. Instead, often, the smallest of conflicts becomes a nuclear bomb that we can not come back from. We do not come back from it. The organizers I knew ten months ago at the start of the genocide are not the ones that are around today, with very limited exceptions who are barely holding on.

We must plan out how we move in and out of organizing. It is my responsibility to build infrastructure. It is my responsibility to ensure the way I am doing my work does not cause more harm in the long run.

Years ago, when I started organizing and mobilizing I believed that it was my responsibility to the movement to show up all the time, regardless of my own needs. I felt that if I did not show up, I had failed everyone who is more marginalized than me. For me, it was my responsibility to die for the movement.

I have learned since then that my responsibility to the movement is not about my relationship with it, it is about strategically building movements that shift us towards a liberated world. Martyring myself so I can feel better is coming from my ego and is not to the benefit of the movement. My responsibility is to take care of myself so that I may be able to be efficient and effective and I can see as much of this work through as possible. Saying that we can't take breaks comes from our ego, not protectiveness for the movement. In fact, it leads to harming it, often resulting in community violence. Don't take out people with you because you're not comfortable taking breaks.

Taking care of ourselves, potentially in the form of taking breaks, is essential and is part of our responsibility to the movement.

Planning my exit from organizing is very similar to transition-planning in any role.

I assess the work that I am contributing to the role/movement. This is a wonderful opportunity to assess what it is I actually do vs what I intended to do. If I intend to focus on community care but I am 90% focused on direct action then this is something I must be aware of.

Ask yourself, what am I currently doing? What did I want to do? What does the movement need right now?

This is also an opportunity to potentially shift the direction your work is heading in.

What is the impact of your work not being done?

Who else can do this work?

The focus here is on organizing skill-building, not necessarily taking on a basic task. There is a part of this that's a little trickier to analyze, and that's how the movement is shifting every day. Ultimately, you're letting go of labor that may be irrelevant by the time you're letting go.

At the very beginning of me doing this work, when I have the most energy, I begin mapping this out. Ideally, this is not something you do when you're already exhausted and about to tap out.

As I collaborate with others I am always thinking about who I should invest in so that the labor is able to be spread between multiple individuals. I am incredible, and there is a lot that I can do, AND a lot of people are incredible and there is a lot that they can do.

Another thing to keep in mind as you're doing this work is capacity. If you are only looking to people whose capacity is already maxed out to take on your labor, you set yourself and others up to be harmed. This is why it is critical to tap into individuals that may not already be in the movement or might not have the right skill sets yet.

This labor is reciprocal. It is like a healthy form of supervision. You must invest in the people around you. If you don't there will be no one ready to take the labor from your plate when you are leaving.

Another aspect of letting go is being willing to shift your contributions and roles within the movement over time. My work should not look the same a year into a genocide. Sometimes I am a leader, other times I am backend support that no one will ever know about. Sometimes I am an educator, sometimes I am a student. My roles are constantly shifting to meet the needs of the movement. Forcing the movement to adapt to our individual desires alone is also fueled by our egos. At the end of the day, as much as we all matter, the movement and the larger community always matter more and are the priority.

Finally, you may need to leave without a replacement. Sometimes, it is still more strategic for some work to stop than for you to continue in your role causing harm to yourself and potentially others.

Plan out your time away and find your way back when you're ready. We still need you.

Yearning for Utopia

Yearning for Utopia: The heartbreak and dream of a better world

Is it wrong to yearn? To dream?

I feel closest to my people when I close my eyes and yearn for more. I feel closest to the land beneath my feet, any land when I close my eyes and bathe in the warmth and pain of a land that has only ever known blood. A land, and people, who know that life is blood and from the blood rises innovation and prosperity. Allah Kareem (God is generous), my people say as our blood is spilled, as our bodies nourish the earth, as settler colonizers move in above our ceilings claiming we were never there. I dream because when I close my eyes I can see their closed eyes looking above, a smile spread across their faces because they know that Allah Kareem and it is nothing for Allah to turn someone's floor into a ceiling and a ceiling into a stairway to heaven.

In this life or the next, my people say. So I dream of Utopia. I yearn for more than what this world has given us, because Allah Kareem and it is only a matter of time.

I came into my understanding of Utopia as a child. My parents and our community stood for an Islam and justice that enveloped everyone. The toppling of empire, the rise of justice, and the creation of Utopia were always a moment away to them. I am eternally grateful for the hope of Utopia they embedded deep within the foundation of everything that I am. I grew up in protests for Falasteen, Kashmir, Northern Ireland, and so many more.

Post-9/11, as community members began disappearing, so did that hope. That hope turned from being shouted on the streets of downtown Phoenix, and organizing space in our masjid, to being uttered in a whisper watching Al Jazeera. As I came into my being, I realized that hope is not readily available and the majority of people believe in limited possibilities and belief systems that do not include Utopia.

I was marginalized as a dreamer long before I ever came into my gender-queerness. My marginalization existed across my displacement, my brownness, my Global South passport, my disability and neurodivergence. And spread across them like embroidery was hope. I learned that it was appropriate to drown in shame and never in hope.

For a moment, a few years into organizing mutual aid and healing justice work I forgot about hope in the midst of the Nonprofit Industrial Complex. I forgot my people's conviction that Utopia is around the corner and at the end of every street. I remembered as I launched my own nonprofit, and then forgot under the pressures of funding and community acceptance. Then I remembered again, months before COVID-19 started. COVID-19 removed the barriers that prevented so many from recognizing just how bad things had gotten. I was able to respond in my people's ways, where there was room for Palestinian decolonization in the chaos of uncertainty. I initiated a mutual aid hub in the state I was living in at the time, bringing together nearly a thousand people to create a system of support that encompassed over 100 municipalities. I launched transformative justice and decolonized healing academies and worked on building infrastructure for our community. In the process, I forgot that death is always near us, and in the midst of dozens of death threats and 18-hour work days for six endless months I ripped myself from the fabric of organizing in the US and found myself in Northern Ireland.

It was on this break, as I did a Masters in Conflict Transformation and Social Justice, that I was able to fully take a step back from the everyday impending-end-of-the-world and think through what a better world would look like if it was built by and for us. The "us" I refer to are the trans queer folks, those at the margins of all marginalization.

During my dissertation I was able to engage with a few other queer and trans Muslims to discuss what Utopia would look like for us and who it would be built by. Since then I have been able to facilitate larger spaces of queer and trans folks to talk about the practicality of Utopia building. This work is not introducing anything new, it is recycled from countless other theorists, predominantly Black and Indigenous Women of Color who have been leading this work since the beginning of human time. We have short memories and these blueprints are often hidden from us, and I hope that my work honors the work of everyone before me and brings these blueprints back to the surface.

Audre Lorde tells us "Revolution is not a one-time event. It is becoming always vigilant for the smallest opportunity to make a genuine change in established, outgrown responses; for instance, it is learning to address each other's difference with respect."

This to me is the foundation of Utopia Building. Utopia is not a one-time event, there is no single event that will get us there. Utopia is in the everyday, and through my work in over two dozen countries and my learning of countless other blueprints—to me building Utopia is not just possible, it's probable if we make fundamental changes to our lives.

In my work, Utopia building is distilled into core values that build Utopia today and every day. These values are hope, love, spirituality, and belonging. These four alone are able to transform any part of our community when they are truly achieved and become a part of the fabric of our everyday lives.

Hope

*there will come
a day when
the sun sets on
a world and rises
in another
where indigenous
sovereignty
is honored
where queerness
no longer
exists
where transness
is no longer
an identity
where humanity
means something
genuine*

-"Amal" excerpt from *Blood Orange* by Yaffa

Part of my background is as a Certified Peer Support Specialist. As part of the foundation of Peer Support, we honor that hope is a necessary tool to support individuals on their journeys for moving past mental health and substance use challenges. Hope is transformative, a guiding force going beyond what is ordinarily seen as possible. Without hope our lives stagnate, we lose purpose and forward momentum. Hope is so powerful that it can be shared and held collectively by a community. In peer support we say a core part of our role is to hold hope for individuals, especially when they are not holding hope themselves. Holding hope collectively allows us to give ourselves and others grace in this work. Some days we might not be feeling that Utopia or anything at all is possible, and that is wonderful. Sometimes we need to be in a space where we feel like nothing will get better and along the way find the things that inspire us to claim hope. In the meantime, a community that holds us and holds hope is able to serve as a reminder of what we have to look forward to and that we are valid and that we deserve better.

Recently, in community spaces I facilitate, I have been asking "what is hope when it is non-attached to an outcome?" Hope devastates when we pretend like we control the outcome. We control our actions, our reactions—but the outcomes are beyond us. We do not know when Falasteen will be free, when Sudan, the Congo, Haiti, Armenia, Kashmir, etc. will all be free, but it can happen at any moment. We do not take an action in this moment because this is the action that frees us. That, we do not know. We act because it is the right thing to do. We will be free, that outcome is not ours.

Love

"There can be no love without justice..."
-*all about love,* bell hooks

bell hooks builds off Scott Peck's definition of what love is "'the will to extend one's self for the the purpose of nurturing one's own or another's spiritual growth.' Love is as love does. Love is an act of will–namely, both an intention and an action."

If we operate our lives from within this definition, then Utopia unfolds around us. Love is not simply a personal and/or an interpersonal practice. Love is a foundation for community building and operates every aspect of our lives. If we took this definition into our relationship with ourselves, others, and into every sector of our lives, what would our lives look like? If a workplace was built on a foundation of love, what would that look like? As we begin imagining these things we realize that a workplace built on a foundation of love can not exist within capitalism. A financial system built on a foundation of love would look nothing like our financial systems today. Instead they'd be filled with mutual aid and reciprocity. Everything would look different. Love in this regard then becomes a tool for transformation and Utopia building.

I began learning the practicality of this definition on my mental health journey, as I was finding ways to live with and navigate CPTSD, body dysmorphic disorder, gender dysphoria, suicidality, and so much more. I was never taught self love or to cultivate self-esteem. The first time I came across the words self-esteem at the age of 23, I knew that this was an entirely foreign concept and required me to build it from scratch. Around the same time, I was developing a relationship with my inner child and learned that loving myself is the same as loving this child. In the last seven years I have rarely had any negative self-talk or even self-doubt, because the love I have for that child is endless. My inner child is perfect, which automatically means that I am valid in everything that I am regardless of what the world looks like. Seeing that I am valid, always, meant that I was able to see that with others. When everyone is valid there is unlimited grace and acceptance for who they are and the journeys they are on; when I am valid I live my life in a way where my outside world also validates this. In my everyday life I do not accept anything less—in my work, in my relationships, in everything. The society around me might be founded on systemic oppression, but every day I get to divest from it and demand better. Knowing that I am worthy of Utopia is transformational.

Spirituality

What inspires me to love? As a survivor of childhood abuse I have often wondered this. Years of abuse and yet a surprising amount of love for my abusers. I still remember when Chris Brown was physically violent to Rihanna. I remember the pain of understanding and knowing her pain in a multitude of ways despite still being a teenager. At the same time, I questioned society's response. A response where Chris Brown was canceled and most people pretended as if this was a unique incident that rarely occurs, without any pathways for healing and community transformation. Years before I knew what transformative justice was, I questioned why it was not a reality in our communities. My ability to humanize individuals who caused me immense harm speaks to my connectivity, which is the definition for my spirituality. We are all connected. Regardless of roles we play in our day to day lives, we are all entwined, and we all have the same building blocks.

Maya Angelou shares words from the philosopher Terrence, saying "I am a human being. Nothing human can be alien to me." She goes on to explain that internalizing that statement means that we all have the building blocks to commit any atrocity AND the building blocks that our heroes have, whoever they might be. Connecting with every ingredient within us means connecting to every ingredient out there—raw star dust and atoms that exist within everything in creation. In connecting with myself, I connect with the land underneath my feet, the land that mourns loss, and the skies that hold endless possibilities. When I am connected I am eternally loving of everything and everyone, most of all myself. Loving myself means I am also protective of everything I am and I work to build the community around me that feeds my soul in a harmonious and ecstatic balance. Because I am whole, so is everyone else. Everyone is whole in Utopia.

Belonging

I belong everywhere. For years I have struggled to belong anywhere when I can not be home. The same home that Darwish asks in a poem, "what in life is worth living for?" and the answer is always Palestine. As a displaced individual I have struggled with being accepted for everything that I am when the land beneath my feet is mourning the loss of Indigenous sovereignty. I have struggled with what my role is at the intersections of displacement and settler hood. Over time I began defining belonging as being accepted for everything that I am or can ever be. For years, my programming has been to build spaces of belonging and cultivating foundations for belonging to be possible.

If belonging is being accepted for everything that I am or can ever be, whose acceptance matters? Is the acceptance from the privileged or the marginalized or the land underneath my feet or myself or the stars or a higher power? Who is it that I desire this validation from? Over time I realize it is not one or another, it is a discomfort of being accepted for everything I am knowing full well that so many others are not. I am warm in spaces of belonging within my community, in particular queer and trans Muslim community, and yet I know that for countless individuals they are not held through community and are only held outside of it.

To cultivate belonging is to begin laying the foundation for how we are in Utopia. There is no marginalization in Utopia. There is no queerness in the sense that no one is punished for who they are. No one is invisible. Everyone is home, in every sense of the word. Building spaces of belonging today allows us to feel what Utopia feels like. When I am in queer and trans Muslim spaces, in particular in MASGD these past couple of years, I am home. My displacement has not disappeared, but within me, through belonging, I have the power to have many homes that live within me and within these spaces of belonging.

Belonging is necessary to build hope. Spirituality is essential to building a loving community. Love is essential for belonging. Hope is essential to building spirituality. These four go hand in hand, and no systems of oppression can survive them.

I yearn for Utopia, and even more so, I yearn to build with others. Utopia is not mine, it is not for a single person or community, it is for all of us.

I read the names of cousins, second cousins, and third cousins on lists procured because "the leader of the free world" said "...I have no confidence in the number that Palestinians are using." In the last three weeks, every one of my identities has been weaponized as a way to justify my people's genocide, my genocide. You might wonder, how can I think of Utopia as the world is falling apart? It is as the world falls that it is made anew. As a death doula, I know that death is a beginning. Mourn the old world and usher in a new one. Let it be a better world.

Acknowledgements

To everyone who has encountered liberatory practice, past, present, and future, I am grateful for every influence and form of support.

To those thanked in previous books, thank you for your continued support.

And to everyone who will never be thanked for their labor in building the revolution, thank you.

Author Biography

Photo by Michael Colgan

Mx. Yaffa (They/She) is a disabled, autistic, trans, queer, Muslim, and Indigenous Palestinian. As Executive Director of the Muslim Alliance for Sexual and Gender Diversity (MASGD), they have earned multiple awards for their transformative work on displacement, decolonization, and equity. Yaffa is also an engineer, peer support specialist, death doula, birthing doula, and yoga teacher.

They are the author of *Blood Orange*, a poetry collection on displacement and colonization; editor of *Inara: Light of Utopia*, an anthology by queer and trans-Palestinians; and author of *Desecrated Poppies* a poetry and essay collection about the connections between anti-trans and anti-Palestinian politics. Their new book, Letters from a Living Utopia, will be released in May 2025.

Yaffa is also a visual artist, showcasing their work worldwide at festivals and art galleries. Yaffa will debut their one-person show, Harvesting Olives, created with support from Rad Pereira, in NYC, October 2024.

www.ingramcontent.com/pod-product-compliance
Lightning Source LLC
Chambersburg PA
CBHW022144160426
43197CB00009B/1418